THE LAW OF ATTRACTION

Little Instruction Book

by Jen McCarty

*I dedicate this book to
the 144000 ~Star seed Twin Flames.*

Introduction

This is a book of miracles, a tale of timeless truth, and a promise to the most ancient part of ourselves to Remember and align with the highest vibration of who we are.

This is your eternal self knocking at your door, coming forth to you with exceptional gifts from The Unseen realm, to share with you all today.

There are gifts and promises encoded in these pages that will, if you allow them, unlock the timeless wisdom you carry within you.

I created this book 10 years ago and this is the anniversary edition. This book was inspired by a show I watched whereby all of the teachers from the "Secret" shared their knowledge.

We are all master creators, and we create everything we see and experience in our physical reality from the predominant thoughts *and feelings* we send out. We are vibrational beings, much like a radio transmitter; whatever we experience as our reality is a direct reflection of the frequencies we emit.

We all possess innate powers to manifest the health, wealth, relationships and careers we desire, and the fastest way to actualise this is through a dedicated and regular practice of Gratitude. To utter a prayer of Gratitude is the most intelligent action we can take, as we have all been infinitely blessed by our creator selves with the gifts of joy, happiness, and profound levels of wealth.

All of these gifts that have been bestowed upon us are completely unconditional and are ours every time we choose to be grateful.

"Gratitude will speed you through your growth and success more than any amount of hard work ever can." ~ David Cameron Gikandi

Happiness is a choice, joy is a choice, fulfilment is a choice, and we all have free will to choose those emotional states in every single moment.

We truly have within us everything we have ever sought, and the fastest way for us to experience it on the earth plane is to be grateful for it, even before we can see it with our physical eyes.

As one of the greatest teachers of the law of attraction, Wallace D. Wattles, said: "It requires power to think of health when summoned by the appearance of disease, or to think riches when in the midst of the appearance of poverty, but he who acquires

this power becomes a mastermind. He can conquer fates, and he can have what he wants."

We are here on this earth to become masters of our mind, and to direct our flow of thoughts to that and *only* that which is positive and for our greatest good. If a thought feels good, then we are in alignment with our heart's desires and if a thought feels bad, we are rapidly moving away from the manifestations of our heart's desires.

As masters of our minds, we are the ones who host these thoughts, these visitors to our holy home, and we eternally have the power to choose to say: "No, you will not enter this holy mansion, you are not welcome

– goodbye" or, as the famous author and speaker Wayne Dyer says to the negative thoughts that knock at his door, "*NEXT!*".

The poet Rumi was right when he said, "This being human is a guest house" and we, as our master selves, are the hosts. We live in a rich, plentiful and happy kingdom, internally and externally. Everything is ours for the taking: truly all we must do is… Ask.

For it already is. That which we seek is already within us – for surely as night becomes day, that which we have tasted, drunk, and known within us, will now manifest into the physical form. It can be no

other way. As above, so below. As within, so without.

Therefore rejoice. Rejoice that all of the riches of happiness and true wealth is ours now, unconditionally, at this moment.

Our time on Earth is precious, and we all have a sacred mission to fulfil that is unique to us. We are here to align with this sacred mission and to take actions to actualise it. We do this by being a fierce gatekeeper against any negative thoughts that try to slip in through the front or back door. Negative thoughts do not serve us or the planet in any way and are a waste of our precious time.

It is much more advisable to spend our time visualising our goals, our dreams, and our intentions for our life, holding a clear vision of all that we wish to manifest… knowing that, in truth, we already possess it! We are then required to let our vision go, and allow the universe to bring our heart's desires to us. It is not our job to wonder how we will actualise our vision; we must be in 100% trust that it has *already* manifested. Then the universe will guide us with inspirational actions and intuitive hunches that will lead us directly to our intended desires.

You will find that this book touches on subjects such as Quantum Physics,

Gratitude, Positive Mindset, Miracles, Power Statements, and more.

We all hold within us the ancient knowledge of who we are. Our purpose is to awaken and to remember that we live in a benevolent and abundant universe – that we will find true flow when we follow our bliss. All we are required to do is focus our intentions, create visual goals (eg. vision boards) and feel gratitude, to bring anything we desire from the unseen realm into physical existence.

The secret isn't a secret at all. This immense creation of which we are all a part is the most spectacular playground our master selves could have ever created. This experience of

being human is truly magnificent. We each hold the key within us to unlock eternal happiness, joy and fulfilment. And the place where it can be found is a most sacred place, as it is forever ours, unconditionally safe and protected. It is within us, and to access this nourishing well, all we have to do is simply to choose it in every moment: choose to be grateful, choose to rejoice, choose to smile, and choose to trust.

Thus we become masters of our minds. In making these choices we take our rightful place as our master self and command that this physical matter become what we wish it to be.

It really is time to wake up – we have all been sleeping for far too long now. Through our own imagination, we access the mind of God. We hold the key to the manifestation of heaven on earth. And the key is simply a choice we make in every moment to be grateful, to be truly grateful, to be positive, to choose happiness purely *because we can.*

And so we find that all along we possessed the key to our heavenly Mother and Father's Mansion; we, as daughters and sons, automatically receive our divine birthright – which is that all of the riches of the kingdom are already ours. We must now simply Ask – then we will receive our inheritance

of unlimited abundance on every level of existence.

Happiness is the golden chalice we've all been seeking; happiness is a smile, a chuckle, a laugh, and the intent to keep choosing it, alongside with gratitude. Then we shall truly understand the holy words "My cup runneth over". We are all God in physical form, so we may as well smile and create greatness everywhere we go.

You will find in this book a number of extremely powerful affirmative statements regarding the true essence of who you are… and a number of quotes on the law of attraction from people such as Albert

Einstein, Lao Tzu, Rhonda Byrne, Jack Canfield, Nikola Tesla, Confucius, Picasso, St Germain, Michael Beckwith, Will Smith and Paulo Coelho to name but a few. (Where a quote is not credited the source of the quote is unknown or the words are from me.)

All of these amazing people and many more including Plato, Galileo, Beethoven, Abraham Lincoln, Thomas Edison and Henry Ford have worked with the law of attraction to bring about some of the greatest achievements this planet has ever known.

Thus it is through allowing ourselves to trust in that which is inherent in us that we can

experience the nirvana of being awake in the Holy Mansion of our Mother/Father God.

We have everything we could ever wish for and so much more: that is the nature of the universe. We can all achieve our wildest dreams, fulfil our life's work, and be happy. We were born as sons and daughters of the Most High. And it is through our IMAGINATION that we have access to all of the riches in the kingdom. That is the key: our imagination is quite literally the mind of God. And being one with God, *we already have everything.* All we have to do is focus our vision and intention on specifically measurable things and we will bring them

forth into the physical earthly plane and experience that as our dreams coming true!

For you to get the most out of this book, my recommendation is to read it slowly in one sitting and then open it up randomly at any time in your day when you wish to realign with your true eternal self.

Life has blessed me profoundly with the gift of unconditional joy, happiness, fulfilment, good health and an abundance of wealth, and this book is one of my gifts back to life.

It is my heartfelt wish to inspire you to the utter depths of your being that you may truly

awaken and claim your birthright as a son and daughter of the Most High.

Truly, we are all so deeply loved and cherished by our master self and there is nothing in this universe that we do not have – everything is already ours for the taking… So let us all remember to Ask, Allow and Receive.

"Therefore I say unto you, What things soever ye desire, when ye pray, believe that ye receive them, and ye shall have them."
~ Mark 11:24

"From abundance he took and
still abundance remained."

~ THE UPANISHADS

"Everything is energy, and that's all there is to it. Match the frequency of the reality you want, and you cannot help but get that reality. It can be no other way – this is not philosophy, this is physics."

~ ALBERT EINSTEIN

"If you wish to find the secrets
of the universe think of energy,
frequency and vibration."

~ Nikola Tesla

"Einstein proved that everything in the universe is energy. All energy vibrates at particular frequencies. We are energy too and so each of us is also vibrating at a frequency. Your thoughts, feelings and beliefs determine the vibration and frequency of your energy."

~ Rhonda Byrne

"There is no matter as such. All matter originates and exists only by virtue of a force which brings the particles of an atom to a vibration and holds this most minute solar system of the atom together. We must assume that behind this force is the existence of a conscious and intelligent mind. This mind is the matrix of all matter."

~ MAX PLANCK

"Assume a virtue if you have it not."

~ SHAKESPEARE, *HAMLET*

Prosperity and abundance
are my birthright.

"There is a thinking stuff from which all things are made, and which in its original state, permeates, penetrates and fills the interspaces of the universe. A thought in this substance produces the thing that is imagined by the thought."

~ WALLACE D. WATTLE

"For verily I say unto you, If ye have faith as a grain of mustard seed, ye shall say unto this mountain, Remove hence to yonder place, and it shall remove, and nothing shall be impossible unto you."

~ MATTHEW 17:20

"The Eternal Law of Life is: What you think and feel you bring into form; where your thought is, there you are, for you are your consciousness; and what you meditate upon you become."

~ St Germain

"Logic will take you from A to B.
Imagination will take you everywhere."

~ EINSTEIN

"When you put your energy, your
vibration, into the air, somehow the
soul of the world is affected."

~ Paulo Coelho

"I study the patterns of the universe and there's a redemptive power that making a 'choice' has. Rather than feeling you're at the effect of all the things that are happening, make a choice. Just decide what it's gonna be, who you're gonna be, how you're gonna do it. And from that point, the universe is gonna totally support you to make it happen."

~ WILL SMITH

"When you want something the whole universe will conspire for you to have it."

~ Paulo Coelho

Name 10 things in your life that you are
grateful for right now.

"Ask, and it shall be given you; seek and ye shall find; knock and it shall be opened unto you. For everyone that asketh, receiveth, and he that seeketh, findeth, and to him that knocketh, it shall be opened."

~ Matthew 7:7-8

"For something to happen so many forces have to be put into action. According to the ancient alchemists and the physicists, everything is one thing. If everything is totally connected, whatever you do interferes with the rest of the world."

~ Paulo Coelho

The universe deeply supports me.

"He who says he can, and he who
says he can't, are both right."

~ Confucius

My happiness is 100% unconditional and based on me choosing it in every moment.

"You can do anything you want to do,
Let your mind, body and soul do it,
Prove it to yourself and say I want, I will, I can.
Do anything…
I know I can fulfil my dreams."

~ INJOY ('90S DANCE MUSIC BAND)

"You are never too old to set another goal, or to dream a new dream."

~ C. S. LEWIS

The one thing that will serve you the most in your life right now is to become addicted to gratitude become addicted to being grateful.

"Anything you can imagine is real."

~ Picasso

"Worrying is pointless and a waste of energy
– it's like walking around with an umbrella,
waiting for it to rain."

~ Unknown

"I wholeheartedly believe that my feelings, dreams, beliefs and ideas are physical in the universe. If we dream something, if we picture something and commit ourselves to it, then that is a physical thrust towards its realisation."

~ WILL SMITH

"The happiness of your life depends on
the quality of your thoughts."

~ MARCUS AURELIUS

"When you focus on something, no matter what it happens to be, you really are calling that into existence."

~ LISA NICHOLS

"Whatever you can imagine is real."

~ NEVILLE GODDARD

"We live in a thought-world, and the world is a part of the thought universe."

~ WALLACE D. WATTLES

"If a universe can be imagined it exists."

~ M. R. FRANKS

I live in a universe of vibrant
health and wholeness.

"Coincidence is the language of the stars."

~ Paulo Coelho

"Life's battles don't always go to the stronger
or faster man, but sooner or later the man
who wins is the man who thinks he can."

~ Napoleon Hill

I am focused on and proactive about my dreams. Today I choose to be happy, because I can! "Imagination is everything, it is the preview of life's coming attractions."

~ Albert Einstein

"The positive thinker sees the invisible, feels the intangible, and achieves the impossible."

~ UNKNOWN

What is the quickest way to make Mother
Father God happy? – Relax.

"Everything around us is made up of energy; to attract positive things in your life, start by giving off positive energy."

~ Unknown

"You can't reach for anything new if your hands are filled with yesterday's junk."

~ LOUISE SMITH

I focus my thoughts, feelings and actions towards attracting and creating health and wholeness on every level – physical, mental, emotional and spiritual. Spiritual wellbeing includes a connection to a higher power, a sense of purpose, intuition, centredness, spiritual practice and service to others.

~ UNKNOWN

"Follow your bliss and the universe will open doors for you where there were only walls."

~ Joseph Campbell

"Throw your soul through every open door, Count your blessings to find what you look for, Turned my sorrow into treasured gold, You pay me back in kind and reap just what you sow."

~ ADELE, *ROLLING IN THE DEEP*

"Imagination is more important than knowledge."

~ Albert Einstein

I am joyous because I choose to be joyous.

The law of gratitude is closely affiliated
with the law of attraction.

"No matter who you are, no matter where you are, gratitude can dissolve all negativity in your life, no matter what form it has taken."

~ RHONDA BYRNE

"Nothing new can come into your life unless you open yourself to being grateful."

~ Michael Beckwith

"Dear universe, I want to take a minute, not to ask for anything from you, but simply to say thank you for all that I have."

~ UNKNOWN

"See yourself as successful visualise yourself
which whatever you believe will manifest"

~ @IAMJOYSPRINGFIELD

"As you focus on sincere gratitude for several minutes at a time, you will move your frequency to one of the most powerful frequencies there is, and all good things will begin to appear in your life."

~ Rhonda Byrne

"The formula for success is to keep the faith,
hold intent, have gratitude, and take action."

~ WALLACE D. WATTLES

"Happiness is an inside job."

~ Unknown

"Let us lay in the sun and count every beautiful thing we can see."

~ NEUTRAL MILK HOTEL,
IN THE AEROPLANE OVER THE SEA

When you realise there is nothing lacking,
the whole world belongs to you.

~ LAO TZU

As soon as we intend something to be, then the universe aligns everything we need to make it happen. We just have to be in trust and gratitude and feel good.

"When you are praising and blessing, you are on the highest frequency of love."

~ Rhonda Byrne

I am willing and able to attract health and
healing whenever I choose.

"A great attitude does more than turn
on the light in our worlds – it seems
to magically connect us to all sorts of
serendipitous opportunities."

~ Earl Nightingale

I am a magnet to love, joy,
laughter and peace.

"Even after all this time, the sun never says to the earth, 'You owe me'. Look what happens with a love like that. It lights the whole world."

~ HAFIZ

"I am the master of my fate, I am the
captain of my soul."

~ WILLIAM ERNEST HENLEY, *INVICTUS*

Whenever you naturally remember to do so, stop thinking… take a short moment to stop your train of thoughts… this one action will lead you to the abiding peace of your true nature…

"Always believe that something wonderful is about to happen."

~ Unknown

"People have a tendency to believe in lack, limitation and scarcity. They may say 'I want a beautiful life' but underneath there's a belief in scarcity. We live in a multidimensional universe. Everything is energy – energy is never destroyed, never created, and it becomes exactly what you put your attention on."

~ Michael Beckwith

I am happy because I choose to be happy.

"Release yourself from being a victim, and
take control of your life's destiny."

~ MICHAEL BECKWITH

"The greatest discovery of our generation is that human beings can alter their lives by altering their attitudes of mind. As you think so shall you be."

~ WILLIAM JAMES

"It's not what can I get, it's what can I give
and how can I serve, and when you're in
that place the universe lines up beside
you and is at your command."

~ JAMES RAY

"Our feelings send out a wave to the universe, and anything that is vibrating at a similar level gets attracted into our life. So if we have a goal or a vision and we focus on that rather than focusing on what already is… we'll attract that."

~ JACK CANFIELD

I have access to infinite power, wisdom,
creativity and abundance.

Today I am expecting and receiving miracles.

My cells are vibrating with love
and ecstasy in this moment.

The sweetest prayer we can utter is a prayer of gratitude for everything. This is an assured route back to Nirvana.

"Write GRATITUDE really big somewhere in your home and whenever you see it, stop for a moment and feel gratitude for something. Really feel it deeply and smile, then still feeling it, carry on with your day. This simple thing can transform your life."

~ LIVING IN LOVE

My body's sole purpose is my wellbeing.

"We have been blinded by our brilliance, ignorant of our genius, and unaware of our true power and magnificence."

~ *THRIVE* (THE MOVIE)

I am now aligning with the wonderful truth
that I am master of my destiny.

"No one makes a lock without a key – God won't make problems without solutions."

~ A. Lynn

"You have become so enmeshed in the belief that you are man that you have forgotten the glorious being that you are. Now that your memory has been restored, decree the unseen to appear, for all things are compelled to respond to the voice of God – your awareness of being. The world is at your command."

~ Neville Goddard

"The substance of this universe is thought. If quantum theory is correct it implies that to change your current reality all you need to do is change the frequency of your thoughts."

~ BILL GOLDMAN

I am deeply supported by the universe.

"Every hour and moment you spend in giving heed to your doubts and fears, every hour you spend in worry, every hour in which your soul is possessed by unbelief, sets a current away from you through the whole domain of the intelligent substance. All the promises are unto them that believe, and unto them only."

~ WALLACE D. WATTLES

"To get something you never had, you have
to do something you've never done."

~ Unknown

"Thought is the only power which can produce tangible riches from the formless substance."

~ WALLACE D. WATTLES

I am deeply grateful for all the blessings I have and all the blessings I am receiving.

"It requires power to think of health when summoned by the appearance of disease or to think riches when in the midst of the appearance of poverty, but he who acquires this power becomes a mastermind. He can conquer fates, and he can have what he wants."

~ WALLACE D. WATTLES

I am the creator of my reality.

My will is all-powerful. I give thanks that I
have manifested my intentions.

Do your future self a favour and be like the White Queen in *Through the Looking-Glass* and believe 'as many as six impossible things before breakfast'.

"What 10 things are there in your life
right now that make you smile?"

~ UNKNOWN

"Each day I am thankful for nights that turned into mornings, friends that turned into family, dreams that turned into reality, and likes that turned into love."

~ UNKNOWN

<u>H</u>ave
<u>O</u>nly
<u>P</u>ositive
<u>E</u>xpectations

"Freedom from the past or anything else always comes the moment you stop thinking about it."

~ MIKE DOOLEY

Today all that is good is available to me.

"Think highly of yourself, because the world
takes you at your own estimation."

~ UNKNOWN

My power is limitless, my joy is limitless.

"Seek ye first the kingdom of heaven within
and all shall be added unto you."

~ Unknown

I am committed to following my bliss.

Today all of my needs are met.

"Worrying does not take away tomorrow's troubles, it takes away today's peace."

~ UNKNOWN

"The hows are the domain of the universe – it always knows the shortest, quickest, fastest, most harmonious way between you and your dreams."

~ MIKE DOOLEY

My life is fulfilling and joyous.

"If you are depressed you are living in the past,
If you are anxious you are living in the future,
If you are at peace you are living in the present."

~ UNKNOWN

"Proceed in full faith."

~ Wallace D. Wattles

"This is the modern interpretation
of quantum theory – that many
worlds represent reality.

~ Dr Michio Kaku

Swim in the ecstatic vibration of
your heart's desires.

During moments of doubt and worry,
I choose to focus on my dreams and visions.

Today I express my genius.

Today I am aligned with the
highest vision of my life.

"The next message you need is
always right where you are."

~ RAM DASS

"I cheated on my fears, broke up with my doubts, got engaged to my faith, and am now marrying my dreams."

~ Unknown

"A human being is a thinking centre,
and can originate thought."

~ WALLACE D. WATTLES

"Don't quit just before the miracle occurs."

~ UNKNOWN

"Serve compassionately, love fearlessly, live intentionally, give thanks increasingly."

~ UNKNOWN

I am willing and able to attract health and
healing whenever I choose.

"There comes a point where you have to step up, put on your awesome cape, and be the superhero of your own life. You are competent, capable and more than enough – you can do this."

~ Choose Happiness

My body flows with energy and purpose.

I am so happy and grateful now that
my body is healed and whole.

I am in control of my thoughts – they
are no longer in control of me.

"Your talents are God's gift to you. What you do with them is your gift back to God."

~ UNKNOWN

I live my life doing things that
bring me great joy.

"We've all made numerous requests to the universe, now all we have to do is feel good about life… to allow those desires to manifest in reality."

~ DONALD B. JUNIOR

"A change of feeling is a change of destiny."

~ NEVILLE GODDARD

"Faith is taking the first step, even when
you don't see the whole staircase."

~ Unknown

"Success is connected with action.
Successful people keep moving – they
make mistakes, but they don't quit."

~ UNKNOWN

Every cell in my body is
pulsating with healing light.

"There are so many people out there who will tell you that you can't. What you've got to do is turn around and say, watch me."

~ UNKNOWN

We know we're on the right path
when we're in bliss and ease.

I remember to remember.

"Turn your cant's into cans, and
your dreams into plans."

~ Unknown

You hold the key to happiness – it's
your choice to open the door.

"Describe the life you want to live, write what it looks like, and what it feels like, then you take action. What action do I need to take to prove to myself that I believe that? The action can be real or symbolic – the mind doesn't know the difference. This recalibrates your nervous system, and speeds up the day where you'll begin to see what you're describing."

~ MICHAEL BECKWITH

"Don't worry, don't be afraid, ever,
because this is just a ride."

~ BILL HICKS

"When the Buddha awakened he laughed."

~ UNKNOWN

Afterword
by Jonathan Cainer

The law of attraction is not just an abstract philosophy. It is a real law and it works every bit as reliably as the law of gravity. With the best possible attitude, in the highest possible spirit, anything can happen. If you 'invite' a positive development into your life, a positive development simply cannot resist the invitation. I have found this to be true time and time again, in my own life and in the lives of those who I professionally advise. This delightful book may seem small but it contains the key to the world›s greatest secret.

Happiness lives in your heart. Unlock it, with gratitude and trust, and it need hide from you no more. Congratulations on making a wise choice. May you make many more.

JOIN JEN'S SACRED COMMUNITIES ON SOCIAL MEDIA

THE EVENT IS HAPPENING TELEGRAM GROUP
https://t.me/Theeventishappening

YOUTUBE JEN MCCARTY COSMIC GYPSY
https://www.youtube.com/channel/
UC_8fJz5gAnhRqZ740QXlzmw

GAB JEN JEN 144
https://gab.com/jenjen144

MEWE JEN MCCARTY
https://mewe.com/i/jenmccarty2

TWITTER JEN MCCARTY144
https://twitter.com/jen_mccarty

INSTAGRAM TWIN FLAMES AND THE EVENT
https://www.instagram.com/twinflamesandtheevent

FACEBOOK THE EVENT IS HAPPENING GROUP
https://www.facebook.com/groups/
theeventishappening

FACEBOOK JEN MCCARTY
https://www.facebook.com/jen.mccarty.75

QR CODES

Please download any free QR Code scanning app on your smart phone and scan the codes below for quick access to Jen's offerings.

4 WEEK SPIRITUAL MASTERY

https://www.jenmccarty.co.uk/
product/4-week-spiritual-mastery-course/

QTTT TRAINING

https://www.jenmccarty.co.uk/
product/qttt-practitioner-training-program/

MP3 ACTIVATION SERIES

https://www.jenmccarty.co.uk/
product-category/mp3-activation-series/

THE EVENT IS HAPPENING MEMBERSHIP GROUP

https://www.jenmccarty.co.uk/memberships

AUTHOR / BOOKS PAGE

https://www.jenmccarty.co.uk/books

HEALY MACHINE

https://www.jenmccarty.co.uk/healy-machine

GLOBAL TRANSMISSIONS

https://www.jenmccarty.co.uk/product/global-transmissions/

Printed in Great Britain
by Amazon